"I've discussed this [...]
who have attended their fair share of galas and the way Dean engages the crowd and brings the energy is like none other. My current Board Chairman had never been a fan of auctioneers until he experienced you. You bring the class and the sizzle to every single gala!"

Amanda Yancey,
The Leukemia & Lymphoma Society® Atlanta

"Dean is a great consultant – walking through auction items and strategizing the best way to generate revenue onsite. In addition, he has great rapport with the audience during the live segment!"

Jennifer Lopez Kunkel,
UNICEF USA

"Dean is a fundraising superhero! From ideation to post event review, I've come to rely on his expertise and willingness to try new things, introduce new concepts and expand fundraising opportunities in the interest of the youth we serve!"

Monica Pantoja,
The nsoro Educational Foundation

PADDLES UP!

My Benefit Auctioneer
REVEALS POST-2020 GALA FUNDRAISER SECRETS

DEAN CROWNOVER
BENEFIT AUCTIONEER SPECIALIST

Crownover Enterprises, LLC
Atlanta, Georgia

Paddles Up!
My Benefit Auctioneer Reveals Post-2020 Gala Fundraiser Secrets
by Dean Crownover

Published by Crownover Enterprises, LLC

www.MyBenefitAuctioneer.com

Copyright © 2022 Dean Crownover

Book Design by Clarity Designworks

Cover photo by Reagan Powell/West Destiny Drive Photography

ISBN 978-0-9785425-1-1 (paperback)
ISBN 978-0-9785425-2-8 (ebook)

Printed in the United States of America

First Edition

I dedicate this book to:

Everyone Working for a Nonprofit

to Make the World a Better Place!

TABLE OF CONTENTS

Who Should Read This Book ix

Introduction xi

Chapter One: The Fund-a-Need. 1

Chapter Two: Live Auctions 17

Chapter Three: Silent Auctions 29

Chapter Four: The Golden Ticket 39

Chapter Five: Sponsorships. 47

Chapter Six: Audience Development 53

Chapter Seven: How to Hire a Benefit Auctioneer . . .59

The Next Step. 63

About Dean 65

WHO SHOULD READ THIS BOOK

According to Candid.org there are approximately 1.5 million 501(c)3 organizations based in the United States. Those nonprofits employ approximately 12.5 million Americans – that's one in every 10 working Americans. If you are reading this, chances are that you are one of them.

First, thank you for all that you are doing to make the world a better place! Where would we be without you?

If you work for a nonprofit organization, especially in development, then this book is for you.

If you have produced a gala or fundraiser for a nonprofit organization, then this book is for you.

If you are considering producing a gala or fundraiser for a nonprofit organization, then this book is for you.

The more revenue you can bring in for your organization, the more they can help others, right?

MY PROMISE TO YOU

You have all the time in the world to read multiple books on fundraising, right? I know you are screaming, "WRONG!"

My guess is that you are overworked and need the right information quickly. With this short, powerful book I'm going to get right to the meat of the matter. Drawing on 12 years of benefit gala experience, I will share with you what I've learned over the last two years of fundraising during the COVID-19 pandemic. No extra fluff or filler!

My book is designed for you to read in any order you like, or just skip to any chapter or topic you need at that moment. My hope is that you find something of value that will help your organization's bottom line. Let me know if it does by emailing me at Dean@MyBenefit Auctioneer.com.

INTRODUCTION

Originally I thought I'd truly be writing this narrative post pandemic. After hosting only virtual fundraisers from March 2020 through May 2021, I appeared at 32 fundraisers during the last six months of 2021 and nearly all were held as in-person events. It looked like we had turned a corner and live events were back.

I have NO virtual events scheduled for 2022. There was a period of uncertainty as the Omicron variant of COVID-19 ran rampant in late 2021 and early 2022. As we neared Groundhog Day I felt like I was in the movie *Groundhog Day* as calls came in from clients about moving dates to later in the year or going virtual. But it looks like we've moved past it now and we can stay the course of getting back in the same room together. The energy of live events is powerful.

I did about 100 events in 2019 – all live and in-person – but when the pandemic hit the U.S. officially in March 2020 all events shut down overnight. What were nonprofits going to do? Their galas were a big part of their bottom line.

Timing is everything. Two pieces of technology were running strong independently already – mobile bidding and live streaming. Luckily for nonprofits, the fundraising world turned quickly to meld these things together and we hardly missed a beat. Many nonprofits saw no halt in donations as virtual galas rapidly became the new normal.

Quickly benefit auctioneers like myself across the nation had to learn this new skill and guide our clients through the process. New best practices were created on the go!

Chad Carvey, *The Principal Auctioneer* in San Francisco, California, a former school principal turned benefit auctioneer, was the first to pioneer a simple, secure and cost-effective Virtual Live Gala technique where the guests bid and donated in the "chat" area of a webinar-style platform. He also taught us how to create a makeshift studio in our homes (his studio was on his boat!).

From Tampa, Florida, Jenelle Taylor aka *Gala Gal* held weekly Zoom meetings for us to discuss new ideas on how to maximize raising money without an audience in front of us. She created a spreadsheet with links to the few virtual auctions that had taken place thus far so we could learn from them.

Scott Robertson of *Scott Robertson Auctioneers* in Ft. Myers/Naples, Florida, upped the game on how a virtual production should look. He hosted a webinar where over 70 fundraising auctioneers joined to learn information they could use in their respective businesses.

And I was one of the first auctioneers on the East Coast to do a virtual event. In fact I had about 24 hours to make my first one happen!

These are just a sample of the auctioneers working hard to keep galas happening. While the world shut down, we worked hard to keep benefit fundraising open.

What we didn't realize at the time was that many new best practices were emerging that would still work on stage when live events were back in full swing.

You are about to learn these best practices that cover almost every area of a gala:

- The Fund-a-Need
- Live Auctions
- Silent Auctions
- The Golden Ticket
- Sponsorships
- Audience Development

As a bonus for those who've never worked with a professional benefit auctioneer specialist, I'll review why that is so important and how to interview one for your event.

Without further adieu, let's go!

THE FUND-A-NEED

Two revenue streams clearly excelled during the pandemic via virtual events – the Fund-a-Need and sponsorships. First let's look at what I consider to be the number one money maker at your event: the Fund-a-Need.

It goes by many names – paddle raise, mission moment, special appeal – but I call it the Fund-a-Need. This is the portion of the gala where I simply ask guests to raise their paddles and donate cash for the cause. I structure the appeal by driving donation levels beginning with the highest ask that makes sense for the nonprofit and ending with the lowest. The most popular levels at my events are $10,000, $5,000, $2,500, $1,000, $500, $250 and $100.

Before the pandemic hit in March 2020, I almost exclusively drove fundraising for the Fund-a-Need at live, in-person events. Its execution is very simple – beginning with an emotional set up I call the *One-Two Emotional Punch*.

One – A short video (2-3 minutes at most) featuring those served by the nonprofit and how donors' gifts enrich their lives. It usually includes behind-the-scenes at the organization and client testimonials.

Two – A live testimonial from a client served by the nonprofit. Typically in two minutes or less, audiences get to hear the personal story firsthand. Not only do guests hear how the organization changed that person's life for the better, they also witness the proof positive of how their donations or gifts make a difference.

Then – I'm the final punch! Once those steps are completed, I take the stage and explain how guests can give. When I call for an amount that a guest wants to give, they simply raise their paddle. I call their bidder number out and it goes onto their tab for that night as a donation.

The Fund-a-Need has increased in popularity over the last decade – especially with major individual donors – as guests want to give more and buy less. Patrons at events tell me all the time that they have enough "stuff". It makes them feel like they are really helping by showing their support at the event and just giving cash. Another bonus: Cash donations are more likely to be eligible for tax write-offs (but talk with your tax consultant to make sure!).

Another great thing about the Fund-a-Need is that you don't have to solicit items to "sell" for it. You just have to tell your story well and ask your wonderful patrons to support your organization with their gifts. In fact, it's so impactful that I have several clients that *only* do the Fund-a-Need at their events. No Live or Silent Auctions. Before virtual auctions, the only limitation was the size of the room and how many people you could get in it to give!

Then COVID-19 hit just as the 2020 spring fundraising season kicked off. Live events of every kind got squashed as the world waited to see what would happen next. Organizations were forced to either postpone their event and cross their fingers for a swift recovery and/or vaccine development, not have an event (and miss out on planned event funds) or go virtual. My clients divided pretty evenly into those three categories for 2020. In fact, many thought they were postponing for a season…and then for another season. But when 2021 rolled around and the world was still a mess, a majority of nonprofits went virtual for the first half of the year because they couldn't afford to skip another year of event fundraising.

Now I see that, in the gala world, we had self-imposed limitations we didn't even know existed until we were forced to appeal to audiences virtually. Moving to a virtual platform blew the roof off of Fund-a-Need giving. It literally allowed us to appeal to a *global* audience and drive donations. While nonprofit organizations have had Donate Now buttons on their websites for years, they had not driven an audience to give the same way they had at their fundraisers *because they had not hosted online galas before!*

When a nonprofit organization creates a virtual gala, they are in reality producing a *television show* rather than a live event. It's a totally different beast – more like a telethon but with modern-day technology. Do you remember the Muscular Dystrophy Association telethons featuring Jerry Lewis? (If not, kids, you can probably find it on YouTube. We saw them every Labor Day growing up a hundred years ago.) The difference is that this telethon is livestreamed on the internet rather than the television network and its success is heavily reliant on the mobile bid platform. Most development teams had not had experience with this type of event until COVID forced them to try it. I told my clients: Realize that your job is now to create a dynamic 30-minute television program, not a four-hour gala.

For the virtual Fund-a-Need, the setup is more or less the same as a live event. During the lockdown, however, we had strict limitations on who could be at a studio – so both the "video" and the testimonial portions were pre-taped.

The biggest difference between driving cash donations at a live event and at a virtual event was in the collection of funds. No longer could I ask for the audience to raise their bidder numbers because there was no audience in front of me. They were out there but we couldn't see them.

As part of the benefit auctioneer community, I worked with clients, colleagues and mobile bidding companies to discover options for the Fund-a-Need that would work well virtually.

Early in the virtual process, mobile bidding companies did not have technology that allowed us to go level by level. That came later – and kudos to them for making it happen so quickly. The version of the virtual

Fund-a-Need that worked best for me and many of my fellow specialists was the *Time Limit*.

The Time Limit is where we set a time limit, usually three minutes, and tell the viewers to give at any level – from a dollar to a million dollars! Using the mobile bidding app, we have suggested levels that match the levels we want to highlight. There is also an "Other" space where they can put in any amount.

While the clock counts down, I discuss with the Executive Director (or similar) what the guest's gift at each level could do. For example, "If you give tonight at the $1,000 level, you could send four kids to camp."

Between levels we also thank donors as their names come across our monitor. That is always my favorite part! Not only is it a terrific way to thank people for supporting you, it actually creates an urgency for other guests to give and builds the competitive energy in your virtual room.

We tell viewers to give throughout the whole show and then reveal the total raised at the end of the show.

NEW BEST PRACTICES

I guess Plato (love that guy) was right about necessity being the mother of invention. We created the Fund-a-Need virtual appeal out of necessity until we were able to be back together in person. In doing so, we developed some great new best practices that I now advise my clients to incorporate into their in-person live events.

Introducing the Fireside Chat

As I mentioned earlier, at a live event, I advise doing the *One-Two Emotional Punch.* This includes a short video followed by a live testimonial before I secure donations from the audience. Done right, it is incredibly impactful. I have also added an element (a third punch?!) that really seems to connect with the audience – the *Fireside Chat.*

Pre-COVID-19 lockdown, the auctioneer usually did most of the talking when collecting donations at live events. In my case, I would discuss how the various levels of gifts could help the organization and then call out the bidder numbers as donors raised their paddles for each level. For me, something fantastic came out of moving to a virtual program. I realized that presenting the need as a topic of discussion with the Executive Director, or someone else who could speak for the organization, added a whole new level of importance. Instead of talking *at the audience* we could talk *with them* – almost like a fireside chat minus the fire. I feel like this method better engages the audience than a single talking head and I have incorporated it into my shows.

Let's talk about how to set up your Fund-a-Need levels. First you need to understand the formula!

Follow the Fund-a-Need Formula

The Fund-a-Need is the centerpiece of your fundraiser and I will always strive to make it more impactful. Years ago I developed a system for my clients to help them pull out important facts to share with the audience – something to highlight at each giving level. I created this simple three-part formula as a tool to craft the perfect facts for your appeal:

Dean's Formula

THE PROBLEM
+ YOUR NONPROFIT'S ACTION
+ YOUR DONOR'S SUPPORT
____
= THE PERFECT "Food for Thought" FACT

1. **First, share THE PROBLEM – a negative "Did You Know" fact**. This is a fact or statistic about the population you serve that communicates the negative – in other words, an issue or problem that your organization strives to remedy. Pick the ones that will really connect with the audience.

   Example: ***Did you know that one in 10 kids go hungry in Atlanta every night?***

2. Next, add an **ACTION** – a tidbit on what **your organization is doing to combat The Problem**. This is the **statement of hope** on how your nonprofit is making a difference thanks to the guest's donations.

   Using the example: ***BUT, thanks to your donations, last year our organization went from serving 10,000 to over 30,000 meals to area children.***

3. Finally, if applicable, add what **THE DONOR'S SUP-PORT** at this level could do.

    Continuing our example: ***Your donation at this level tonight could feed 100 kids next month!***

I work together with my clients to craft the right messages to share with the audience from the stage to drive their gifts. In the past, it was just me on stage delivering the message. The difference now is that we present the message to the audience, live or virtual, in the more engaging Fireside Chat format of a question-and-answer session. It goes something like this:

> **Dean:** *"Ladies and gentlemen – Did you know that one in 10 kids go hungry in Atlanta every night? BUT, thanks to your donations, last year our organization went from serving 10,000 to over 30,000 meals to area children. Ms. Executive Director, explain to us why the need is so important right now."*

> **Ms. Executive Director:** *"In the last year we've had over 1,000 requests for meals within our Feed-A-Child program. That's a 201 percent increase from 2019. With every dollar raised we can buy nine dollars in food for our organization."*

> **Dean:** *"Amazing! Your donation at this level tonight could feed 100 kids next month! Now, who will donate? Hold up your bidder numbers!"*

When the virtual auctions seemed to be winding down in 2021 and we were going back to in-person events, I wondered if this dynamic would work well on stage. I'm thrilled to say my audiences and clients love it!

The key to success is to deliver the message in a timely manner – short and sweet – so we don't lose the audience. I coach the person I am working with to keep their answers to the script we discussed and not to exceed 30 seconds. Less is more. We don't need to preach to the guests; we just offer food for thought so they feel motivated to give.

I encourage you to create a Fireside Chat for your next event and see how your audience responds. Share your experiences at Dean@MyBenefitAuctioneer.com.

Fund-a-Need Best Practices

The Fireside Chat is only one of the great ideas that came out of virtual events. Let's talk about some of the best practices you should consider doing, too, whether your event is live or virtual. Below are the key actions I recommend:

Start the Fund-a-Need Early

Pre-pandemic, the success of the Fund-a-Need was limited by how many guests we had in the room. When we went virtual, we opened up the opportunity for the whole world to give.

Virtual events showed us it made sense to open the online event early. Because the virtual show itself is so much shorter than a live event (best practice is 45 minutes compared to a three-hour event), we began opening the online platform early to offer more time for guests to bid and give. Plus, it allowed flexibility for those unable to tune in "live" more time to give.

With your live event, the same rules apply. Open giving through your mobile giving website the Saturday before the event. This will allow those who cannot be at the event to give. You'll be surprised how much you can raise even before the event night! I recently had a client raise nearly $30,000 in pre-giving. That's huge and it helped us push way over our goal on event night.

More on this in Section 3: Silent Auctions.

Assign Item Numbers to Your Giving Levels

On your mobile bidding website, create each giving level as a catalog item: For example, item #101 is the $10,000 Fund-a-Need giving level. This makes it easy for your donors to find their giving level and easy for you to market – all you have to do is refer to the item number.

Consult with your mobile bidding company on how to do this. I like for the 100s to be the Fund-a-Need giving levels, the 200s to be the live items, the 300s to be silent items and 400s everything else. This setup makes it easy to explain to guests and to track throughout the event.

Describe the Giving Levels

Create a description for each giving level that matches what you will say in your Fireside Chat on stage. It doesn't need to be word for word but include the essential information. For example, the catalog description may simply say, *"Your gift of $1,000 could send four of our wonderful kids to camp with all expenses paid."*

Make sure you have pictures of those you serve as part of the description. In the case of the children going to camp, show your donors happy kids playing on a ropes course or swimming – something that shows the positive impact of their giving.

What about a quote from someone you've served? Further showcase your impact by including that direct message. For camp, for example, you may include a quote from Sam S. of Decatur, Georgia: *"I love going to camp! It's the only time I can yell inside and out and not get in trouble!"*

Always include something like this at the bottom of your giving level description, too: *"Can't attend the gala? Please give now and your gift will be included in the final tally on event night. Thank you!"*

Put the Fund-a-Need First

Where you put the Fund-a-Need in your run of show at a live event will directly impact your profits.

In the past, a typical run of show may have looked like this:

    6 p.m.   Doors open
    7:30 p.m.   Seated for dinner and welcome
    8:30 p.m.   Awards and speeches
    9 p.m.   Live Auction
    9:45 p.m.   Fund-a-Need
    10 p.m.   End program

In the last few years, I have seen that holding the Fund-a-Need after the Live Auction puts some clients in danger of missing out on serious donations. Guests started leaving before the end or, frankly, by that time were sometimes too drunk to give. I never want to leave money on the table! Once I defined the problem, I joined a small group of benefit auctioneers that were breaking with tradition and putting the Fund-a-Need *before* the Live Auction. That group has grown over the last couple of years and seen exponential revenue growth. Here's why.

Not everyone can afford the Live Auction. In fact, at any given event only about 20 percent of the audience can afford to buy those high-ticket items. That leaves the other 80 percent out. If you put the Live Auction first, they may leave their seats to mingle, go to the bar or even go home. And getting the audience back in focus after the craziness of the Live Auction is like herding cats. You can forget it!

With the Fund-a-Need, 100 percent of the audience can give. Putting that as the heart of the show – before they are too tired, bored or drunk – allows them all to participate. I recommend placing it at a point during the event when they are alert, seated and focused on why they are there and why their gift matters. The Fund-a-Need can band people together to make a big change for your organization.

As we make this change, clients often ask: "If we have the Fund-a-Need first, what if guests leave during the Live Auction?" To that I say – those who leave were not going to bid anyway. Maybe they gave during the Fund-a-Need. Or they were part of the 80 percent who could not or did not want to buy a live item. It's okay if they move around or go home. I am only interested in those bidding – and those bidders stay put.

When I work with a client, here's how the run of show for a typical seated dinner looks:

6 p.m.	Doors open
7:30 p.m.	Seated for dinner and welcome
8:15 p.m.	Fund-a-Need
8:30 p.m.	Live Auction
9 p.m.	Awards and speeches
10 p.m.	End program

Notice that awards and speeches are last. Why? **They don't make you any money**. When was the last time you heard your tablemate say, "Boy, I hope they have more speeches!" Never. Of course, there are exceptions to all rules – and that will be for another book – but I hope you see the importance of putting the Fund-a-Need early in your program.

Keep It Open After the Event

You will make a bulk of your Fund-a-Need donations at the event...but hold it open for gifts longer. Ask guests to send the message to their base of friends and colleagues to help raise more for your critical mission. Doing this is very simple.

At the end of the live event, after I raise all I can from the folks in the room, I announce that we are keeping the Fund-a-Need portion of the auction open for another week. I ask guests to check their emails for more information. The organization sends out the link on where to give the next day or the following Monday when they send their Thank You email to guests. I once had a school make another $10,000 by doing this! It cost them absolutely nothing but a little time to craft the email.

KEY TAKEAWAYS FOR THE FUND-A-NEED

- Use the Fund-a-Need Formula to create the most empathic levels you can.

- Make the giving levels easy to find on your mobile bidding website by assigning item numbers and descriptions.

- Open online giving a week before the event and keep it open at least a week after the event.

- At your live event:

  » Put the Fund-a-Need before the Live Auction and earlier in your program.

  » Begin with an appeal I call the *One-Two Emotional Punch* – a short video followed by a live testimonial.

  » Create a Fireside Chat to give more food for thought to your audience. Talk *with* them, not *at* them.

LIVE AUCTIONS

For an in-person event, the Live Auction is considered the main part of the show. It's where the big ticket *items* meet the big ticket *buyers*. A good show has drama, comedy, suspense and several elements in between. Did you know that statistically only about 20 percent of an audience can afford the Live Auction? So – it's a spectator sport, too! It has to be entertaining to keep your audience tuned in and participating. And it was, until it all crashed!

Overnight in-person galas turned into virtual galas and suddenly securing tangible auction items became a huge hurdle. As the pandemic took its toll on businesses, many businesses stopped donating as they didn't know what the future held – and, sadly, some shut down altogether.

What did nonprofits do to make up for the loss of donated items?

In the absence of donated items, many nonprofits opted for **more consignment items**. These are prepackaged trips and experiences that you buy from a reputable company like HGAFundraising.com, TuscanResort.com or MitchStuart.com. These companies charge a fee for each trip called a *reserve price* (their hard cost for the item). There's not an upfront cost but, once the item is sold, the consignment company collects their reserve price for each trip sold. For example: A donor wins a trip to the Caribbean for $3,000. The nonprofit's cost is $1,500 for the trip, so they have "raised" $1,500 on this item.

While consignment trips helped, the big problem was that the world basically shut down and travel was not even an option. Donors weren't sure when normal travel would be possible. Nonprofits had to come up with other things to sell.

Popular items became **focused on experiences** that could happen from a distance or even in a family or community pod – like beach houses, Zoom experiences with celebrities, etc. For instance: I sold a 30-minute Zoom chat with a popular Georgia politician for close to $15,000!

Driveable getaways where families could quarantine themselves became huge sellers, especially beach houses. If you are going to be locked in, rubbing your toes in the sand and basking in the sun sure helps make up for the pain.

SELLING LIVE ITEMS VIRTUALLY

Once organizations acquired some desirable items, the question became: How do we sell these items virtually?

There were no people in the room, no paddles being raised, no bid spotters to help generate the excitement and energy during a hot bidding war… But, after some trial and error, we developed some best practices for selling live items virtually. Because technology to sell items virtually in real time (as if people were bidding against each other in a physical room) was not quite there yet, we started treating our Live Auction-worthy items like Silent Auction items.

Like the Silent Auction, the live items were put online for bidding a week before the event on the organization's mobile bidding platform. We highlighted "live" items, listing them in a category named PREMIER or FEATURED, and made it a point to market them constantly. The goal was to get those bids up high before we live-streamed.

Then what used to be the Live Auction portion of a live event became the *closing countdown* for these featured items. When it was time during the livestream to "sell" them, I started an imaginary timer telling the guests they had three more minutes to bid. I used that program time to highlight the items I was shutting down – usually two or three items at once per three-minute period. The countdown generated some excitement and virtual bidding wars as people got in their final bids – and then I could call SOLD. We got creative using platforms like Facebook and YouTube for nonprofit chat coordinators to thank donors as guests put in their bids, answer questions and even help generate some of the playful banter online.

Now that some of the virtual smoke has cleared, a few lessons and best practices have emerged clearly. You can use these at your in-person events.

Less Can Generate MORE

When I first started auctioneering in 2008, it was not uncommon to have 10 or more items featured in the Live Auction. I know auctioneers who were selling 20 plus items onstage at a gala! Consider that it takes three to five minutes to describe, generate bids and close the sale on a big ticket item. So, multiply your number of items by five minutes…and you're at an hour with 12 items! That is a long time to expect an audience to sit and pay attention. Remember, only a small percentage of the audience can afford to bid in the Live Auction, so a majority of your guests would be getting ancy.

It became clear even before we went virtual that audiences do not want to sit through a long Live Auction. Over the last few years, I've seen a steady decline in the number of items put in the live program – from 10, to eight to six…and today, I recommend focusing on three to five high-quality items during your live program. That's a 15- to 25-minute quick, fun Live Auction that can yield a high return but not cause a majority of the audience to bail or head to the bar.

So, a major lesson from a post-virtual auction world – less can generate more! It's quality over quantity. Don't throw things in the Live Auction just to sell them. Craft that Live Auction with your audience in mind.

Which items do you pick, you ask? That leads me to something I've been preaching for years…

Mine the Data

Think of your auction this way: You are a "store for a day" and you need to sell your items out in less than three hours. As an added stress, you need to sell them over fair market value. To do this you need to stock that store with what your clients are eager and excited to buy. Luckily, like any retail business, you probably have data from past events so you can see how your items performed.

So, MINE THE DATA! Meaning, look at what has sold in the last few years for the highest amount. Then look at its fair market value. Do some quick math and get a percentage number. Did it sell close to or over fair market value? If so, get more items like the ones that sold well. Simple. You want to have the trips, experiences and items that your particular supporters want. Don't worry about other galas and what they sold – yes, you can get ideas from them but they don't dictate your event. Pay attention to data from your ongoing supporters at past events to show you what worked and what didn't.

But what if it's our first gala and we don't have data, Dean?!! Fair question and easy answer – ask your guests what they want.

I've spent hours in meetings watching committees debate what they should have in their Live Auction (and Silent Auctions, too). One day I asked a committee if they polled their guests on what they wanted. Everyone looked at me with a blank expression. Instead of trying to guess, I suggested that they send out a survey to their top supporters and ask what they would be most likely to buy. I invite you to do the same! And, by the way, whether this is your first event or not, asking advice from your top supporters is a great way to engage them in your mission and your event! Every touchpoint is an opportunity for fundraising. (My wife made me say that.)

Create a very short (two-to-three question) survey asking things like:

What is the number one trip you have on your bucket list?

What is your favorite restaurant?

Where is your favorite place to vacation that is within driving distance?

Keeping it short will encourage more responses. And, after enough surveys come in, you will start seeing common threads. Now you have clues about what your guests will engage in bidding wars to acquire. Use this input to guide your acquisitions!

Ask for Longer Expiration Dates

Here's something else we learned from 2020... Ask supporters to donate items to your event that allow for longer expiration dates.

Over the years, the typical expiration date has always been one year from the time of the gala. In other words, you get the winning bid on something and you have one year to redeem it. During the COVID-19 world, though, guests didn't know when the coast would be clear to travel or enjoy that chef's experience or spa day or – *insert other cool thing that involves people being close together here.* That expiration date became a big hurdle. What if guests did not bid on an item because they couldn't use it within a year? I advised my clients to ask the donor if they would honor a 18-24 month expiration instead. Almost all of them said *yes*!

Going forward, I still suggest that you ask for extended expiration dates. In the past, the expiration date was listed as a restriction – but now, an extended expiration can be highlighted as a feature for that item. With the barrier of a short expiration date lifted, buyers get excited knowing that they have time to use it, and their bids will reflect that!

Preview Live Items Early

In the past, guests typically learned about the live items at the event itself. This did not always give them enough time to explore the items and get emotionally invested. After all, once you are at the party, there are a lot of things going on and it's easy to miss out on the primary reason for the event – supporting the mission **financially**.

Even more than the pandemic, the rise of mobile bidding in the last decade also made it easier to pre-market items and create excitement long before people entered the door. Couple that with the forced movement to a virtual platform in 2020, and this best practice became a necessity.

Virtual or in-person, prepping the bidder is crucial to your event. All items need to be listed on your event website and you should feature live items in your emails and other pre-event marketing. Because the live items will most likely be sold at your in-person gala (and assuming you are not hosting a true hybrid event – meaning both bidders in the room and virtually can bid in real time) you should display your Live Auction items as Preview Only on your mobile bidding website. This allows guests to read all about the items but not bid on them like they can on the Silent Auction items. **Bidding for live items is reserved for only those in the room**.

Launch your mobile bidding website at least 5-7 days before your event – preferably a Saturday by high noon. This allows your guests to have plenty of time to get acquainted with the live items, nay, to get excited about your items to the point where they will not let anyone outbid them! I'll share more about this in the Silent Auction chapter.

Be Detailed

Would you spend thousands of dollars on a big-ticket item without all the features and fine print? Probably not. Assume your supporters won't either – so give them all the information they need to bid high. I've been working with my clients for years to make sure they can feed me ALL the details to really drive bids from the stage, especially on their premier live items. I want to be so knowledgeable on those items that I can answer any questions potential bidders may have. But before I take the stage and sell, it is your job to make sure bidders are informed by including a detailed listing on your event site.

In the past, clients were limited by space in their print marketing – printed programs, posters and emails. In the digital world, however, you have plenty of space to include all the perks and restrictions for items. Think of yourself like Amazon when building your catalog! The more information, pictures and reviews they have on a listing, the more likely a buyer will take the chance. The same is true at your auction – an informed bidder bids high.

Include the following with your item listing:

- **Pictures! Pictures! Pictures!** Especially if it is a vacation. Ask the donor for as many as they have. The more professional, the better. If using a consignment company, they should have plenty for you to use.
- **Videos** – Does the item already have a promo video? Embed it in the listing. It will market itself!
- **Link to a Website** – If the item has a website, like a VRBO listing for a vacation home, put it in your listing. There the bidder will get plenty of information that you don't have to track down. And, as a side bonus, you are marketing that item for future sales for your donor which is a great way to encourage repeat business for them and repeat donations for you!
- **The Good** – List all the perks of the item. Going off our vacation example: How many bedrooms and bathrooms? How many people does it sleep (that is often different than how many bedrooms because there are sleeper sofas, bunks, etc.)? How many balconies? Is there a pool? Walking

distance to the beach, shops and restaurants? Beach toys and chairs to use? Wi-fi? Washer and dryer? List the top amenities that will get them hooked.

- **The Bad** – I am a big fan of listing all restrictions like expiration dates, blackout dates, cleaning fees, airfare not included, etc. Respect your bidders by letting them know the parameters. They will thank you for it. You don't want a call later from a supporter who is disappointed that they got an unexpected charge or had a bad experience that could have been prevented.

- **A Note from the Donor** – This is a tip I heard recently that I love. Have the item donor write a short quote or make a quick video sharing why they love supporting your organization. This reminds the potential bidder that they are not just buying an item but are supporting a great cause.

KEY TAKEAWAYS FOR THE LIVE AUCTION

- Audiences have short attention spans. Aim for three to five highly desirable Live Auction items knowing that it takes about five minutes to describe and sell a Live Auction item.

- Mine your data to find out what your guests find highly desirable for the Live and Silent Auctions. Also, identify which of your supporters spend the most!

- Survey your guests on what they want you to sell at the event.

- Ask for longer expiration dates – at least 18 to 24 months is best.

- When you launch the Silent Auction on your mobile bidding site, make sure you are previewing the Live Auction items, too.

- Be as detailed as possible when writing your auction item descriptions – add the good and the bad (i.e., the features and the restrictions).

- Consignments are packages (trips and experiences) that are sold to the nonprofit at a set price called the **reserve**. These can help you acquire highly desirable items IF you cannot secure them as donations.

SILENT AUCTIONS

When it comes to galas, the Silent Auction is the most familiar revenue stream. Almost everyone who has ever been to a fundraiser has participated in this moneymaker. It's simple to understand, fun and offers items at different price points that allow more people to engage.

Many clients have a love/hate relationship with the Silent Auction. They love it because they know guests will love it, it will bring in some money and the Silent Auction displays can make great decor. They hate it because it is the **hardest revenue stream to fulfill**. They have to ask for items, store the items, haul the items around, display them at the event and then try to sell them over fair market value. That requires a lot of energy – especially considering that the average Silent Auction only brings in about 50 percent of its total fair market value.

Even before the onset of the pandemic and the rise of virtual galas, organizations were beginning to limit their Silent Auctions as they recognized the amount of work required compared to the ultimate financial pay-off. As I said earlier, I'm a big fan of looking at your data to determine where to spend your energy. Many times after comparing how a client's Silent Auction performed to, say, their Fund-a-Need – which required *a tenth* of the work to organize – I see the big "Ah Ha!" moment in their eyes.

I am not suggesting that you cut your Silent Auction altogether but I will say that its scale has changed. **It is not the number one revenue stream**. In fact, it's often the *fourth* money-maker after sponsorships, the Fund-a-Need and the Live Auction. It is important that you understand the potential low return on investment (ROI) so you can concentrate your focus and limited human resources on your top money-making generators.

Now, Silent Auctions actually did very well in 2020 and 2021 when organizations had to push virtual events. Silent items performed quite well in most cases – still not better than the Fund-a-Need and sponsorships – but well. Knowing that organizations were in a tough place and had to cancel their in-person galas, patrons really came through to support them. They were buying everything they could, and often over value. I saw gift cards, which have a set fair market value (versus a perceived value like other items), often sell for 200-300 percent of value. As we have returned to a "somewhat normal" in-person gala season, I'm seeing the Silent Auction return to its normal performance.

Here are a few of the best practices related to the Silent Auction we learned from our virtual performances.

LET THE WHOLE WORLD BID

Before, organizations were bound by the guests in the room when it came to bidding in the Silent Auction. When the world shut down and nonprofits went virtual, we sought a wider audience of bidders. As discussed earlier, the mobile bidding platform made it easy for anyone in the world to participate. Many organizations had already obtained auction items before March 2020 so the only downside was working out how to distribute items post event – whether it was arranging contactless pickup or by shipping to winners out of state.

Today, you do have to go get items, store them, market the heck out of them and distribute them – but the important thing is that you open the Silent Auction up to everyone. Not only is it a great opportunity to get more and higher bids but you may even attract new long-term supporters. I now encourage clients to open up the Silent Auction and the Fund-a-Need to everyone via their mobile bidding platform. Share your mission far and wide!

Open Bidding a Week Before Your Event

We have lifted the restriction of event-time only bidding. In the past, organizations had a set number of guests in a room and a set amount of time to educate them on the opportunities to bid. There is not a lot of time to get bidders emotionally attached to your beautifully selected and laid out items – which is the key to a bidding war. Add to those challenges that guests are at a party and want to drink, eat and chat with each other and, well, you can imagine the missed opportunities.

Thanks to a best practice used virtually, you can combat these restrictions by launching your mobile bidding site a week before the in-person event. This includes your Silent Auction, Fund-a-Need, any raffles and your Live Auction preview. Doing so allows your guests to get excited about your event and to start bidding and giving – to get skin in the game early! Bidders will have time to really study your packages, talk about them with friends and partners and start getting emotionally attached to them. Get the buzz going so that your supporters want that item and will not want to be outbid!

From the Fund-a-Need chapter I repeat: ***Dean's rule is to open bidding by noon the Saturday a week before the event***. Why the Saturday before? Simple, that's when people are typically most relaxed and not rushed. Maybe they are finishing a late breakfast when your email or text comes in saying your mobile site is now open for bidding and giving. They will spend the weekend and into the following week doing just that.

Opening early also allows you to to send emails throughout the week highlighting certain Silent Auction items. Draw attention to the ones that need bidding and the ones that already have bidding wars. In my opinion you can never over-market your items. Don't hold back on inviting your supporters to engage.

When you start bidding early and warm up your guests in this way, you will walk into your event with bids on most items. Then you can focus on the race to end the bidding on event night. Use the countdown to motivate your guests: They've had all week to bid but now it's closing down in X amount of time. If they want to win they need to bid!

But, thanks to virtual, there is now an alternative practice you can consider.

Consider Keeping Silent Items Open Longer

Closing the Silent Auction on the night of the event is the most common best practice. It allows you to get those items sold and distributed to the winners onsite. However, some clients now yield additional profit by keeping the Silent Auction open until noon the next day.

Many of my virtual clients did this and it was a hit. There was no rush to close it the night of the event because there were no guests present. We closed the Live Auction items but kept the silent open.

Here are some "pros" and "cons" of this practice:

- **PROs**
  - » #1: First and foremost, you have a chance to drive more revenue by allowing more time for bids post event – after guests have gone home and realized "Man, I really do want that amazing experience!" Several clients raised thousands of dollars extra by keeping it open until the next day and sending emails to drive those final bids.

  - » #2: If anyone missed the event either in-person or virtually this gives them time to still bid and participate.

» #3: You don't have to bring all the items to the event. This will save you time and energy when it comes to transporting and displaying the items. You can arrange a time later in the week for the guests to get their winnings. I really recommend it to schools because they are a built-in distribution center. Parents are there several times a week so picking up won items is easy.

- **CONs**

  » #1: Sometimes it's easier to close the Silent Auction down that night because most of your supporters are there as opposed to watching virtually. I had several clients, after looking at data, realize that when they went back to an in-person auction that almost all their supporters were coming to the event and not watching it online.

  » #2: Sometimes clients want to see items displayed live. While item details are now online, there are some items they may get more excited about when they can see them up close. Think about that basket of a million cool items that looks way more impressive live than in that single photo.

  » #3: You have to deal with the items one more day after your event and sometimes you just want to be done!

It's worth discussing with your committee on whether or not this is the right choice for you.

Host Smaller Silent Auctions

Over the last few years the number of items in the typical Silent Auction has decreased. **It's about *less* making *more*.** That means less items making more profit. Earlier I gave reasons on why the Silent Auction can be troublesome – you have to ask for items, store the items, haul the items around, display them at the event and then try to sell them over fair market value – but there is one more important reason they are getting smaller: so you can have BIDDING WARS!

When you have highly desirable items, having fewer of them can push increased bidding. If you have too many packages, you dilute the auction and your guests get overwhelmed trying to keep track. I once had a client tell me that the year before they partnered with me they had 500 guests and over 500 Silent Auction packages! And, guess what? Those items did not bring in anywhere close to their fair market value. I also find that large Silent Auctions are often padded with less desirable items that don't get bids at all.

The formula I recommend to determine the maximum number of packages to have in your Silent Auction: ***30 percent of the number of guests attending is the maximum number of packages you should offer.*** So, if 100 guests are coming, have no more than 30 packages. Why? Assume that most of the guests coming are couples so, if 100 guests are coming, that's closer to 50 "wallets" in the room. Having fewer packages (as long as they are highly desirable items) allows those 50 wallets to focus their bids and get emotionally attached to those items. Instead of the three or four bids you may get on an item, you'll be setting yourself up for 10, 20 or even more bids on that package. Less items means less work on your part but more profit for the organization. One, two, three, four, I smell a bidding war!

Display Fewer Packages

Another great thing we learned from virtual events: you don't have to set up a physical display for *every single* Silent Auction item. There are no physical displays with virtual auctions so we had to ensure the mobile bidding site had all the details for every item and great photos or images to pull in the bidder. Opening the site early for viewing and bidding also allows your supporters the time to get very familiar with all the items.

Even though we have returned to in-person events, you don't need to go back to physical displays for all of your items at the event. Your guests will continue to view items online, and they can start bidding the week before. I recommend displaying packages that have a WOW factor live – like posters for a fabulous trip, a beautiful piece of art, or a basket with fantastic items in it. For example, I have a client who got a basket from a TV network full of so many unique things from their shows you couldn't even list them all. Seeing a photo online wasn't the same as gazing through the three-foot tall basket covered in cellophane and bulging with all kinds of unique media and pop paraphernalia!

You don't have to create a display for things like gift cards, teacher experiences or dinners. Guests can read all of that on the bidding site. This creates a lot less work for you and your team.

For those items that you do display, make sure you do the following:

- Place the packages in a high-traffic area so all guests have to walk by them.
- Put the item number from your mobile bidding site on the display description. It's easier for guests to look up the package by its item number than to type in keywords. Most mobile sites let you print out the description and automatically add the item number.
- Have signage that reminds your guests that the displays represent a sample of the items being offered. They should go to the site to view all items.
- Send marketing emails promoting the silent items you want to make sure they see.
- Have the Silent Auction closing date/time on your marketing signs, printed program and bidding site.
- If you are closing your Silent Auction on event night, make sure you have the items at the event ready to give out to the lucky winners.

KEY TAKEAWAYS FOR THE SILENT AUCTION

- The average Silent Auction brings in 50 percent of its fair market value.

- Launch the Silent Auction (along with the Fund-a-Need, raffle tickets and Live Auction preview) a week before your event – preferably on the preceding Saturday at noon.

- Market to your whole database that the Silent Auction is open and that you need not be at the event to win.

- Consider keeping the Silent Auction open until noon the day after the event (review the pros and cons first).

- To push bidding wars on highly desirable items, the number of packages you offer should equal approximately 30 percent of the number of guests coming to the event.

- Mine your data to find out how Silent Auction items have performed for you in the past. Only repeat those that have done well.

- Consider physical displays for fewer of the packages at the event. Thanks to mobile bidding, you don't have to display every item.

- Include item numbers in your marketing so guests can find things easily online.

THE GOLDEN TICKET

Adding revenue streams like raffles can bring in more income, offer lower set price points for guests to participate in, and they add some interactive excitement to your event. When we went virtual we couldn't do tried and true in-person games. This forced us to rely more on raffles and drawings and unique ways to engage audiences. From my experience, virtual raffles performed very well – especially the **Golden Ticket**.

Note that raffles are usually considered a game of chance and may require a license. Check with the gambling laws in your area to determine if you can do a Golden Ticket. The revenue you generate may be worth the license process.

WHAT IS THE GOLDEN TICKET?

Traditionally, the "Golden Ticket" is a raffle where the winner gets to pick one of the Live Auction items to take home free and clear. It's usually priced at $100 per chance and the winner is drawn right before the

Live Auction. The item that the Golden Ticket winner chooses is then taken out of the Live Auction and the remaining live items are sold. It's a very popular raffle because it allows guests who may not be able to afford (or just wouldn't bid the full amount on) a live item the chance to take one home. It is thrilling for the audience and extremely profitable for your organization when done right.

During the pandemic, the Golden Ticket became a real challenge as my clients had a difficult time getting quality items donated. That's where consignment companies saved the Golden Ticket. As I explained in the Live Auction chapter, consignments are packages (trips and experiences) that are put together by a company and sold to the nonprofit at a set price called the "reserve".

HGA Fundraising, a vacation consignment company I work with often, came up with a brilliant idea to help clients during this difficult time. They took five of their travel offerings and created their own turnkey Golden Ticket option. Instead of what may be a lackluster offering of donated items in the Live Auction, some of my clients held a separate Golden Ticket offering the HGA Fundraising items. We still sold our donated items via Live Auction but the new version of the Golden Ticket helped supplement the Live Auction as a separate raffle.

This offering cost the organization $2,000 (the set reserve price for the winner's choice of package) so they only had to sell 20 tickets at $100 to break even. Anything after that was pure profit for the organization.

Because HGA's items were so high-end, like an all-inclusive trip for two to the Caribbean or a Tuscany trip that includes a cooking class and wine tastings, it helped get guests to tune in and participate. They are still offering it and it's a big hit. They've even added another version that has higher end, more luxurious prizes. They advise selling those tickets at $250 each.

Then another version of the Golden Ticket emerged. Instead of giving the winner a *choice* of packages, we offered only one super high-end item (usually a vacation) and guests bought tickets for a chance to win it. One of my long-time clients used a home in Mexico that had several bedrooms and a full-time staff, including a chef, as the prize. The reserve price from the consignment company they chose to use was $6,000 so they needed to sell 60 tickets to break even. In the end they sold about $22,000 in tickets so, after the consignment fee, they still made $16,000. Not too shabby!

Do the Math

With any variation of the Golden Ticket, the key is to do the math before you decide to add it as a revenue stream. Take either the consignment price you are paying for the prize or the highest valued item (if you are letting the winner choose a prize) and divide it by $100. That's your break-even price. **You must sell at least that many raffle tickets**.

Why the highest value? Because you are assuming that the winner will choose the most expensive item and you want to be ready for that. For example: You have five items in your Live Auction and the beach house is the highest valued at $3,000. You must sell 30 tickets to make its fair market value.

On a side note: **By law only the donor can state the fair market value of an item**. Not you! When obtaining the item from the donor, please ask them to value it. That is how you get the fair market value for your donations.

But Dean: That high-valued item could have brought in 100 percent from a single buyer in the Live Auction.

Could it? Maybe, maybe not. Most live items in my experience bring in anywhere from 75 to 200 percent of fair market value – it depends on the item and the "wallet size" of the buyers in the room. The ultimate goal is getting it over 100 percent of fair market value. When you offer a Golden Ticket that most guests can afford, the revenue you make from it covers what a single buyer would have paid for it and then some.

In the example I shared with the house in Mexico: The item cost the organization $6,000 and made $22,000. They generated 267 percent from that item. I'm a great seller (if I do say so myself!) but even I would be shocked if I had gotten $22,000 from a single buyer for it. Collectively the item was "purchased" by several buyers each paying $100 but only one actually got to take it home.

Let the Whole World Buy Tickets

One of the reasons that raffles like the Golden Ticket and its variations proved so successful during virtual auctions: we could offer raffle tickets to everyone in the world. I recommend this as a best practice as we continue in-person. You are no longer bound by how many people are in the room but by how many of your supporters you can get to buy tickets.

I advise offering the Golden Ticket on your bidding website as soon as you can – even before the Silent Auction and the Live Auction items are up. Oftentimes guests will buy one or two when they are buying their ticket to the gala. As long as you know what the prize or prize choices are, you can start selling them. Check with your mobile bidding company on the best way to do this.

My client that sold $22,000 in tickets created a campaign targeting every supporter, donor, friends of donors and beyond. There were also 300 guests in the room on event night. We had a team of energetic sellers working the room to sell Golden Tickets as I made announcements throughout the night explaining the Golden Ticket and how to buy it.

During virtual events, I called the winner live on air when we pulled their ticket. Not having a live audience made everyone feel isolated so calling the winners live really helped people feel connected. I'd call the phone number on the raffle ticket to let them know they'd won and to find out which item they wanted (if we were offering a choice). This went over so well with the viewing audience that now I do it at live events if we are selling raffle tickets beyond those in the room. In the case of the Mexico house, the winner was actually someone not attending the event. The live audience loved hearing her over the phone as she screamed with joy. It added a whole new dimension of fun!

KEY TAKEAWAYS FOR THE GOLDEN TICKET

- Consider adding a raffle as a revenue stream at your gala.

- There are several versions of the Golden Ticket including:

  » The winner chooses one of the Live Auction items

  » The winner chooses from items that are separate from the Live Auction

  » Only one great prize is offered

- Do the math and make sure you can sell the amount of tickets to cover your costs or make the fair market value.

- Most Golden Ticket raffles cost $100 per chance.

- Sell tickets to everyone in your database and let them know they do not need to be present to win.

- Abide by all gambling laws in your area.

SPONSORSHIPS

During virtual auctions, two revenue streams really performed – the Fund-a-Need and sponsorships. I thought that the Fund-a-Need would do well because patrons wanted to support their causes during extraordinary times but it was sponsorships that really surprised me. In the heart of the pandemic, sponsors did not pull out or turn their backs on nonprofits. They were there to continue their financial support.

Here's a couple of gems that came from the virtual event experience that I recommend you follow for your live gala:

ENTER YOUR GALA IN THE BLACK

Prior to the pandemic onset in 2020, the general event rule was to sell a certain amount of sponsorships to help reach a nonprofit's overall goal for the gala, perhaps covering 40-50 percent of the event goal – or at least covering the cost of holding the event. When we had to go virtual, however, that changed. First of all, ticket sales went away because there were no in-person events. Then, additional revenue streams like traditional gala games were gone, again, because there were no people gathering to play. Organizations had to look elsewhere for revenue. That's where sponsors came to the rescue.

After the first few months of virtual events, a brilliant auctioneer – Greg Quiroga of *Stellar Fundraising Auctions* in San Francisco, California – noticed that sponsorships kept selling even without all the perks of in-person events. He began advising his clients to try and sell 80-100 percent of their revenue goal in sponsorships *before* the online gala thus entering the event already in (or very close) to profit mode. I agreed wholeheartedly with his philosophy and started advising my clients as well. For many nonprofits, getting $10,000, $5,000 or even $1,000 in sponsorships was easier than trying to find things to "sell" in their auction to raise that much. Eventually many of my clients would tell me they reached their virtual event date already in the black!

Now, I advise the same thing for in-person events. Work as hard as you can to make your revenue goal with sponsorships. Sponsorships are the way you engage some supporters year-round, and acquiring them decreases the pressure on event night to generate everything from your audience.

One side benefit of selling more sponsorships: A more relaxed YOU on the day of the event! My clients walk into the room much more chilled than frantic because they know they already have a big chunk of revenue in the bank for the event.

Sell the Farm!

Traditionally, sponsorship packages have been levels from Presenting Sponsor down to Patron level, each with perks based on the financial investment of the sponsorship level. At live events, top incentives for sponsors are typically based on the number of tickets/seats received, or a guaranteed table. For example, a Presenting Sponsor for $25,000 may get a table with eight seats plus other perks like print or digital marketing for their company and entry to a VIP hour at the event with upgraded drinks and hors d'oeuvres. A lower level, for example, a Patron sponsor for $1,000, may only get two tickets or just their name in the program. There is no rule on what the organization has to offer its sponsors, you build out your sponsor levels and benefits.

Because nonprofit organizations going virtual needed to bump up selling sponsorships, they had to get creative on perks since tables and tickets were out. One of the first things that popped up were **virtual sponsor parties**. I saw organizations team up with caterers (who were also struggling thanks to COVID) that would deliver food and drinks to guests' homes on the day of the event. Then those guests would jump on Zoom for a virtual party right before the show. Sponsorship money covered the hard costs and allowed the organization to make a profit while sponsors could still feel like VIPs and enjoy the party, whether dressed to the nines or in their new favorite leisure wear. From there extra deliverables were offered to the general public for a fee. It became a good revenue stream when you had a virtual auction. I even saw some very clever drive-through pick-up-your-virtual-party-supplies events that felt like parades. All of these things generated great energy while helping supporters feel connected from a safe distance.

From there organizations went all-in on sponsorship levels. They started selling the farm! For instance, some of my clients secured sponsors for every budget line item required to produce their virtual event – like the cost of the studio, the livestream company, the catering for the crew, and for me, the auctioneer. I'm a big fan of this idea!

Now that we are doing live events again, I advise clients to do BOTH: Continue selling the traditional sponsorships as they have in the past but also consider getting specific sponsors for other items. For example, sell sponsorships for the:

- Venue
- Liquor and drinks
- Food
- Sound company
- Decor
- Auctioneer
- Valet company

Another great sponsorship idea from Greg Quiroga of *Stellar Fundraising Auctions* – and one of my favorites: Sell the Refresher Station. Do you know what that is? It's the bathroom! Sponsors of the Refresher Station get a sign in the ladies' and gentlemen's bathrooms with their logo on it.

Your event doesn't have to look like a NASCAR car with logos everywhere. Maybe they only get mentioned online and in the program. Maybe they get a shout out from the stage. It's all up to you! But don't miss the opportunity to generate a tremendous amount of revenue from sponsors before you even walk through the gala door.

KEY TAKEAWAYS FOR SPONSORSHIPS

- During the pandemic sponsors did not turn their backs on nonprofits. They became even more important and continue to be a huge part of live galas today.

- Try to sell 80-100 percent of your revenue goal in sponsorships prior to event night so that you are in profit mode (or close to it) before the doors even open.

- Go beyond the traditional sponsorship levels and sell all components of your event. Get creative and have fun with this!

6

AUDIENCE DEVELOPMENT

Around June 2021 live, in-person events seemed to come back in full swing. From June until the end of the year, I worked with about 30 clients on events and all but four were live. Because my clients wanted to be very careful with their guests and make sure everyone was safe, they invited roughly half or two-thirds the size of the audience they had at their last in-person gala. A tough but necessary action during uncertain times.

No one knew how these in-person events would perform with smaller groups. But something amazing started happening – we raised more revenue with fewer guests! The first gala I performed back in-person, our Fund-a-Need goal was $50,000 – that was half of what we raised at their 2019 event. We raised $99,000! I saw this over and over again – more profit and less patrons in the audience.

Was it because guests were just thrilled to be out in public again? Maybe. Was it because patrons had extra stimulus money to give? Perhaps. Was it because they were totally dazzled by my sequin jacket and even more dazzling wit? Certainly. It could be for any reason but I think the most significant factor was this: Organizations were limited by how many they could invite so **they only invited their top givers**.

There's a saying in my business: *It's not about having warm bodies in the room, it's about engaging those who can attend AND spend.* Meaning – if you want to have a financially successful fundraiser, invite those with the means to give. Yes, I know that some galas are not about making the most money possible, some are about community awareness and what I call "friend-raisers" versus "fundraisers." But this book is about new business practices post 2020 virtual events that will help your bottomline. One of the best practices both pre- and post-virtual involves **cultivating the right audience**.

By the way – smaller attended events can also cost far less than large galas. Organizations can book smaller, less expensive venues, save money on food and drinks, spend less on decor and sound systems, and many other savings. What we learned in 2021 is that, because organizations had the right people in the room, they made more AND spent less.

INVITE TOP GIVERS

In the chapter on Live Auctions, I advised you to mine your data from past events to find out what your guests want to buy. The same idea applies to cultivating your audience for success. Look over your data from the last few years and create a list of attendees that bought and gave the most. Pull this from all of your fundraisers – even those beyond the gala. Look at online donations, direct mail appeals, sponsors, volunteers. Where are your top supporters? Then create a Guest Wish List based on how many you can have at the event and invite them directly.

What about your *top, top givers*? Do you have anyone who came last year – maybe on a free sponsor ticket – and spent thousands of dollars at the Live Auction or in the Fund-a-Need? First, consider giving them free tickets if they are ultra givers/buyers but, more importantly, *call them personally to invite them to the event*. This is an art that is getting lost in the impersonal world of social media and email marketing. **The simple act of picking up a phone and making a 10-minute call could net you thousands of dollars**. Have the highest ranking person in your organization do it, or spread calls out amongst your board members. Let the patron know they are important and thank them for what they have done for you in the past. Every touchpoint is an opportunity for engagement in your mission.

Here's a case in point: I know of an organization that had a very loyal supporter not only buy one of the highest sponsorships but also came and spent plenty of money on items at the event. The next year, about two weeks from the event, I asked what sponsorship he had purchased. Blank stares. It turns out no one had contacted him!

When there are new volunteers working an event each year, there can be a disconnect when transferring information and some things get lost. I happened to know him personally so I called to tell him about the event. He said he had his big donation ready but no one called...so he gave it to another organization. He did end up giving a donation but nothing like he would have had someone called him at the beginning of the planning process. Let this be a lesson to you. Always look at your data and identify your best givers early. Make them feel like part of the family by inviting them personally to your event!

KEY TAKEAWAYS FOR AUDIENCE DEVELOPMENT

- Invite top givers from your database to your event. You want to make sure your supporters who can afford to attend and spend are invited to do so.

- Inviting only top givers for a smaller gathering can reduce your gala expenses.

- Have the highest ranking person at your organization call and invite these givers personally. Let them know how important they are!

HOW TO HIRE A
BENEFIT AUCTIONEER

Raising the most money possible is almost always the main goal for an organization hosting a gala. As you, your staff and volunteers know, it is a LOT of work to plan and implement a really successful gala. You and your board likely have a lofty financial goal for your event that makes it worth the time and expense of hosting the gala (and you constantly remind yourself of that when you're in the middle of the chaos, am I right?).

That's why investing in a benefit auctioneer specialist is one of the most important actions you can take to ensure you make the most revenue possible. **After all, why put in all that time and effort to NOT generate the most money you possibly can to support your mission?**

First of all: What IS a benefit auctioneer? The National Auctioneers Association has a special designation that an auctioneer can achieve – the Benefit Auctioneer Specialist (BAS). To earn this designation, auctioneers must complete 24 hours of additional classroom training, submit a detailed auction summary report and proof of completing six fundraising/benefit auction events to prove their expertise in fundraising auctions. We are also required to complete several hours of ongoing training along with annual fees to maintain our BAS designation.

How do you hire a great benefit auctioneer? To help you find the best of the best, here are the questions you should ask:

1. **Are you licensed in my state?** Many states require an auctioneer to be licensed. For example in the state of Georgia, it is illegal to sell items at any auction including fundraisers unless the auctioneer is sanctioned by the state. It is common for auctioneers to be licensed in several states.

2. **Do you hold the Benefit Auctioneer Specialist designation from the National Auctioneers Association?** I was the first auctioneer in Georgia to achieve the BAS designation. As new ideas, techniques and technology pop up, I also pride myself on being amongst the first to learn and share with my clients. Your auctioneer should be the same.

3. **Do you specialize in fundraising auctions?** There are many types of auctioneers. Some have specialties like selling antiques, equipment, real estate or vehicles. The same is true for auctioneers who fundraise. It's a specialty that requires training

and experience. Not all auctioneers are equal by any means. While some auctioneers can cross over between specialities many prefer to focus on one. I only work with nonprofit organizations and my sole focus is benefit auctioneering.

4. **How long have you been a benefit auctioneer?** An auctioneer may say how long they have been auctioneering in general but you want to know about fundraising. As mentioned before it is a very specialized skill that requires more finesse than speed to command a giving crowd. For instance, I have been a licensed BAS since 2011. Averaging 70-100 clients on any given year sure adds to my experience level!

5. **Do you consult as part of your package?** Here's the biggest difference between a BAS and other auctioneers. A BAS is trained to consult you on all things related to your gala – from revenue streams, items to sell, run of show, marketing, the Fund-a-Need and more. Many traditional auctioneers are "guns for hire" who show up, sell and leave. They may not have a vested interest in making your event the most successful fundraising event it can be. Ask if consulting is part of your candidate's offering or whether you can book it as an additional service. I am an A-Z benefit auctioneer. My clients benefit from all of my knowledge including videos, my *The Ultimate Benefit Auction Guidebook*, an arsenal of emails to guide them through their event timeline, and, of course, several one-on-one meetings including my signature Event Envisioning meeting.

6. **Will you be the person conducting my auction?** Some auctioneer companies send out a person on their team to interview with you and then, once booked, may send another auctioneer to conduct their event. This business model can work very well but make sure you understand who is doing what. I work solo, meaning my clients only get me as their consultant and auctioneer the night of the event. That way I am fully embedded in their goals and objectives.

7. **What is my investment?** They don't teach you in school how to hire an auctioneer! There is no set fee structure but usually it comes down to you paying either a flat fee, a partial flat fee plus a percentage of what is raised or simply a larger percentage of the total raised. Ask your candidate their fee structure and make sure you understand the differences. I am a flat fee so my clients pay one price for everything I do. I used to have different fee structures but over time found that one price works best for me and my clients.

THE NEXT STEP

Thank you so much for reading this book. I hope it helped!

Interested in having me at your next gala? Please schedule a **Fundraising Event Consultation**.

I work very closely with my clients to develop their fundraising strategy, uncover revenue stream opportunities and "auction-tain" your donors from stage so they can't wait to give!

Because I am (happily) booked with repeat clients and have more new inquiries than time available, here's how I choose: I partner with clients that I can help achieve and exceed their event fundraising goals of $100,000 or more.

Are you one of those clients?

Go to www.WorkWithDean.com to tell me about your organization and event.

We will review your submission within 48 hours and, if you are a good fit, we schedule a **Fundraising**

Event Consultation to explore what working together looks like. This consultation will last about 30 minutes.

I want to help you have the most successful event in your history!

ABOUT DEAN

Dean Crownover is an Atlanta-based benefit auctioneer with over 25 years of professional entertainment experience – the last 12 as a benefit auctioneer specialist. His love of good causes and nonprofit organizations shows in his attitude and performance at every event. Dean's popularity soars due to two skills that make him unique – he can control even the rowdiest crowd while bringing in maximum donations and bids. He travels the United States raising millions of dollars for his clients.

His wife, Amy, serves as chief operating officer of My Benefit Auctioneer and edited this book (unless you found any typos, in which case she never saw it). Her previous career culminated in fundraising for Atlanta-based New American Pathways as its chief advancement officer. Dean and Amy have one teenage son, London, who seems to love baseball and Chipotle right now more than anything!

GA Lic #AU003829

www.MyBenefitAuctioneer.com